THE
5 O'CLOCK
BAND

WORDS BY
TROY "TROMBONE SHORTY" ANDREWS
WITH BILL TAYLOR

PICTURES BY
BRYAN COLLIER

ABRAMS BOOKS FOR YOUNG READERS, NEW YORK

Everyone's hometown is special. It's the place that helps you grow into the person you'll become. For one little boy called Shorty, his hometown roots were very important. He was from New Orleans, and in this city, there are sounds and tastes and celebrations unlike any other place in the world.

Many even call it magical. The city showed Shorty how to see the world. And its people helped him become the person he was destined to be.

Shorty liked to play music—in fact, he was in a band. They called themselves the 5 O'Clock Band because that was the time they started playing every afternoon, after school and homework were finished. The band lived in a lively neighborhood called Tremé.

The 5 O'Clock Band would parade through the streets of Tremé, down to Jackson Square in the center of town, and back around, just like all the older musicians did. They played for the people for rounds of applause, and sometimes they even got tips! But one day Shorty was practicing his trombone and got so lost in his own music that he forgot to meet the 5 O'Clock Band at their regular time.

Shorty ran to Jackson Square, trombone in hand, but his bandmates had already left. He had missed their performance and parade, and he knew he had let them down. One day I want to be the bandleader, but how can that happen if I can't even get to the show on time? Shorty thought.

Shorty walked through the neighborhood, around the large square in the French Quarter where musicians gathered. He smelled delicious gumbo and jambalaya in the air and heard the sounds of other musicians echoing through the streets.

But Shorty kept his head down. Not even the sounds of the brass instruments could cheer him up. Until suddenly he heard a booming voice cry out,

"Shorty, **WHERE Y'AT?**"

Shorty looked up to see Tuba Tremé. He was a giant of a man, but he was as sweet as pecan pie—and the sounds that floated out from his horn were even tastier. Tuba and his band had been playing in the Quarter for as long as Shorty could remember, and they played songs that were over one hundred years old.

"WHERE Y'AT, Tuba?" Shorty called back, feeling down.

"Looks like you've got the blues, little man." Tuba Tremé had noticed
Shorty's sad face.

"I missed the 5 O'Clock Band, and I don't know where they've gone.
I'm afraid I won't have what it takes to be a real bandleader
if I can't even show up on time."

Tuba Tremé placed his giant horn to his lips. The first notes of "When the Saints Go Marching In" tickled Shorty's ears. Like so many other New Orleans musicians, Shorty had learned how to play his horn with this tune. Pride swelled in Shorty's chest as he and Tuba played the same notes together that Louis Armstrong had played many years before them in these same city streets.

"**Tradition**," Tuba Tremé said. "Every bandleader needs to know where music came from in order to move it forward."

"If you understand tradition and you keep it alive, you will be a great bandleader."

"Thanks, Tuba," Shorty said as he waved goodbye. He hoped to be able to play just like Tuba Tremé one day.

Shorty continued walking through the Quarter along the banks of the Mississippi River. A steamboat floated alongside him, and the steam whistle sounded. He thought about how many musicians had played on that river. Even Louis Armstrong! Shorty blew his horn back to the steamboat and smiled.

His growling stomach led him back toward home, but the scent of red beans and rice made him stop in his tracks.

"WHERE Y'AT, Shorty?" Queen Lola called out the window of her restaurant. Shorty was still feeling defeated, but no one could refuse a meal from Lola, the Creole Queen, one of the best chefs in New Orleans, if not the world.

"**WHERE Y'AT**, Queen Lola!" Shorty answered as he opened the door. Queen Lola served him a heaping plate of red beans and rice along with andouille sausage, collard greens, and okra with tomatoes. She had been making this dish for over fifty years, treating everyone who came through her door like family—even Martin Luther King Jr.!

As Shorty dug in, he asked Queen Lola the question that was weighing on his heart. "I let my band down today, but I want to be a great bandleader and make amazing music—just like you make amazing meals in your kitchen every day. How do you do it?"

Queen Lola smiled wide. "**Love**," she said. "There's love in my food, because I love every dish I make. It's my special sauce! As long as you love what you do, you will always be a success."

"I don't love anything more than playing music, but this meal sure is close! Thank you, Queen Lola," Shorty said.

"Come by anytime, Shorty." she said.
"Why don't you head back out and see if
you can find your band?"

Shorty felt a little better now that his belly
was full, but he knew he still had more to learn.
As he walked toward Tremé looking for his band,
he heard the rumbling of drums in the distance.
It sounded like glorious thunder! As he turned
the corner, he stood face-to-face with the most
majestic person he'd ever seen.

"We are Indians!" A chant pierced through
the warm, swampy air. It was the chief of the
neighborhood Mardi Gras Indian tribe.
Big Chief and his drummers chanted as
they pounded out a rhythm: "We are Indians!
Indians! Indians of the Nation, the whole
wild creation!"

Shorty knew this song was a prayer that the Mardi Gras Indians sang before they marched down the streets. They believed the song would protect them on their journey as they went through the city looking for other tribes.

Mardi Gras Indians only exist in New Orleans—
they are a special group sacred to the city.

"WHERE Y'AT,

Shorty?" Big Chief asked as his group slowed their drumming.

"WHERE Y'AT,

Big Chief!" Shorty hollered back. "You and the tribe sound amazing. I'm actually looking for my group, the 5 O'Clock Band, but I need to know: What does it take to be the Big Chief?"

Big Chief picked up his tambourine and shook it proudly as he looked up to the sky. "**Dedication**," he said. "Each year, all the Indians make new suits, hand-sewn from scratch. It takes a lot of time and patience, but when we hit the streets, it's worth it. We are the soul of Mardi Gras."

Shorty noticed how Big Chief's suit shimmered in the light. He thought about how important it was for him to practice his craft every day in order to carry the honor of being a bandleader.

Suddenly, Shorty heard the familiar melody of a brass band in the distance and ran toward it. He knew those sounds could only come from the 5 O'Clock Band. And there were his friends, parading down the avenue toward him.

"WHeRe Y'aT?"

the 5 O'Clock Band sang.

"WHeRe Y'aT!"

Shorty answered.

"I'm sorry I wasn't there for you guys today. I promise I'll never let you down again," Shorty said. "But I learned that we have all the ingredients we need for success."

"We have **dedication**. We honor **tradition**. And, most of all, we play with **love**. Now I know what it takes to lead."

"Why don't you start us off and take the lead right now, Shorty?" one of the boys said.

Shorty raised his horn to his lips, stepped out in front of the band, and played the opening notes of "When the Saints Go Marching In."

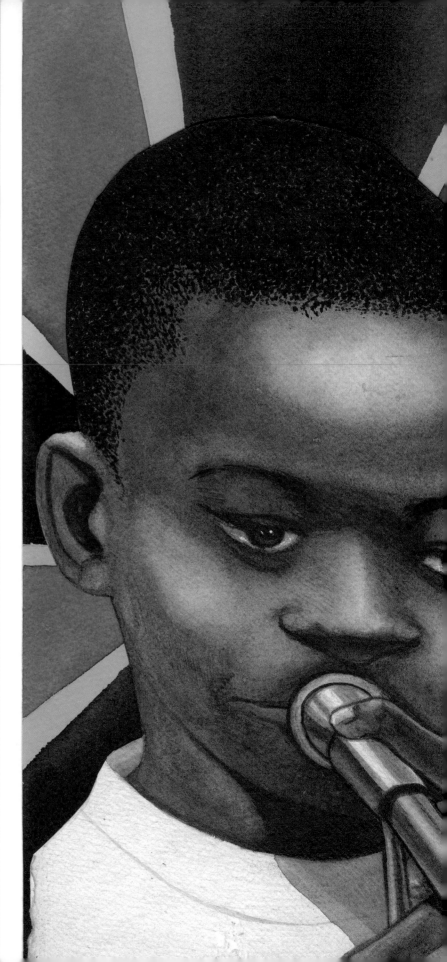

As the 5 O'Clock Band paraded home to Tremé, they waved at the friends and neighbors who clapped their hands and danced in step behind them.

AUTHOR'S NOTE

Before there was Trombone Shorty & Orleans Avenue, there was the 5 O'Clock Band. I started the group with my friends, and we named it for the time when we would gather—after school let out and homework was done—to parade around our neighborhood and play our instruments. In New Orleans, we call this type of musical procession a "second line," and it's a tradition that goes back for more than one hundred years, before jazz even had a name. My friends and I "second lined" every day, parading through Tremé and the nearby French Quarter, just like Shorty and his friends do in this book. While doing that, we received a hands-on education on what it means to be a musician.

We were just little kids then—I was only five years old when we formed the group!—but we were standing on the shoulders of giants, those influential musicians who helped originate, grow, and pass on our New Orleans style of music. We started out by imitating them and learning their songs, but through the power of this practice, we learned who we were ourselves.

I still look up to the legends who've played an active role in the creation of the musical culture of my city: James Andrews (my brother), the Rebirth Brass Band (my cousins), Jessie Hill (my grandfather), Danny Barker, Irma Thomas, Allen Toussaint, the Neville Brothers, the Marsalis family, the Batiste family, Fats Domino, and the king of them all—Louis "Satchmo" Armstrong. They are my teachers and my heroes, along with the many street musicians who I've watched play in New Orleans throughout my life. Thanks to their examples, we learned how to make music, and also how to celebrate life. I've tried to honor them in this book, especially one of my favorite musicians who I used to watch in the French Quarter when I was a child—we called him Tuba Fats.

Courtesy of Troy Andrews

THE REAL 5 O'CLOCK BAND—TROY ANDREWS IS ON THE FAR RIGHT WITH TUBA.

BIG CHIEF JUAN PARDO AND THE GOLDEN COMANCHE MARDI GRAS INDIANS

One of my city's—and our country's—greatest gifts to the world is our music. In New Orleans, we've created musical styles you won't find anywhere else. We also have our own entirely unique culture, built of rituals and traditions that feel as old as our music. Just one example is the Mardi Gras Indians. They are a group of predominantly African American people who dress up or "mask" as American Indians every year during the Mardi Gras season. They make elaborate, hand-sewn suits, embellished from head-to-toe with feathers, beads, and rhinestones. They are organized into multiple "tribes," and the tribes meet in the streets to sing and dance in a mock battle to determine who can create the most stunning performance.

Some say the tradition started in homage to the American Indians who helped runaway slaves. I enjoyed celebrating their rich history and pageantry in this story.

New Orleans takes great pride in its artists and its community, and with good reason. For me, making music represents society functioning at its best. When a group of individuals collaborate in harmony—with sincerity, spirit, and soul—they create something beautiful. They face and overcome challenges. They aren't afraid to dream for the future. Growing up in Tremé, I was encouraged to seek guidance from all the musicians who lived there. So I did.

In late August 2005, everything changed. Hurricane Katrina devastated many places that are so important to our culture. It took years to rebuild after the damage, and some homes, businesses, and entire neighborhoods still haven't recovered. But those that have are back and better than ever, like Dooky Chase's Restaurant on Orleans Avenue, just down the street from where I grew up. This legendary restaurant inspired the one that Shorty visits in this book.

Parts of Tremé are confronting a different challenge—the cost of living here has risen, new laws limiting the performance of live music have been enacted, and many of the musicians who grew up here can no longer afford to stay. I began to worry that music would not be passed down the way it once was.

That's why I started the Trombone Shorty Foundation, to ensure that the next generation of New Orleans musicians has the same opportunities that I did as a kid. Every week, a group of students gathers in Tremé at the Jazz & Heritage Center to receive lessons from members of the Soul Rebels and New Breed Brass Band, two of our great, young New Orleans bands that are passing our musical traditions on to the next generation of aspiring performers.

This book celebrates the ways in which the spirit of community and mentorship can help cultivate the passion and skills that can change a life. It's a story inspired by how my own life was changed by the vibrant culture of New Orleans and by all the mentors who showed me kindness along the way. And that's exactly our mission at the foundation. Hopefully, I can play a role in keeping our culture strong in the lives of children in the same way my mentors did for me.

ILLUSTRATOR'S NOTE

The 5 O'Clock Band is my second collaboration with Troy "Trombone Shorty" Andrews, and I was very interested in providing a more intimate glimpse into the life of the young musicians of Tremé—as well as digging deeper into this special neighborhood.

In this story, a young Shorty takes you by the hand and walks you through his personal world. So I wanted the reader to experience the same tour of New Orleans visually through my artwork. I hoped to evoke the smells of red beans and rice and sounds of a steamboat whistle and horns ringing out in Jackson Square, and to introduce readers to a cast of characters who represent the rich legacy of this town—like the majestic Mardi Gras Indians. All of these people and places connect the past, present, and future of New Orleans culture.

One of my favorite scenes in the book is when Troy and his bandmates march through the street together. On the page, they are as tall and powerful as the surrounding buildings. I think these boys knew that when they played their instruments all together, they were giants. And that is how I wanted to depict them: larger than life.

Today, more than ever, the world needs to know Troy's incredible story of hard work and dedication and his message about the importance of tradition as he continues to spread his music around the world, while always remembering to honor and celebrate his home.

TROY "TROMBONE SHORTY" ANDREWS WITH THE TROMBONE SHORTY ACADEMY

ABOUT THE TROMBONE SHORTY FOUNDATION

The mission of the Trombone Shorty Foundation is to preserve the rich musical culture of New Orleans. The foundation provides music and business education and mentorship to young, talented New Orleans students, known as the Trombone Shorty Academy, while providing them with a vision for the future. Experienced, professional instructors help these aspiring musicians express themselves and pursue their dreams while also supporting their community.

Please visit www.tromboneshortyfoundation.org.

TO THE CITY OF NEW ORLEANS ON HER 300TH
BIRTHDAY—THANK YOU FOR ALL THE PEOPLE,
SONGS, AND TRADITIONS YOU HAVE GIVEN
ME. THEIR INSPIRATION IS WITH ME
EVERYWHERE I GO.
—TA

TO MO AND FIG, FOR TEACHING ME HOW
TO BE A BETTER PERSON EVERY DAY.
—BT

TO ALL THE CITIZENS OF THIS WORLD,
WITH THE HOPE THAT WE SLOW DOWN AND
RECOGNIZE THE INSPIRATION ALL AROUND US.
—BC

The illustrations in this book were made
with pen and ink, watercolor, and collage
on 300-pound cold press paper.

Cataloging-in-Publication Data has been applied for and may
be obtained from the Library of Congress.

ISBN 978-1-4197-2836-5

ABRAMS The Art of Books
195 Broadway, New York, NY 10007
abramsbooks.com

THE TREMÉ NEIGHBORHOOD IN NEW ORLEANS

iStock.com/lightphoto